A Dunn
1996

ELTHAM AND WOOLWICH TRAMWAYS

Robert J Harley

MP Middleton Press

DEDICATION

I would like to dedicate this book to the memory of my father, John Harley (1912-1966).

First published April 1996

ISBN 1 873793 74 X

© *Middleton Press 1996*

Design - Deborah Goodridge

Published by Middleton Press
            Easebourne Lane
            Midhurst
            West Sussex
            GU29 9AZ
            Tel: 01730 813169
            Fax: 01730 812601

Printed & bound by Biddles Ltd,
            Guildford and Kings Lynn

CONTENTS

INTRODUCTION AND ACKNOWLEDGEMENTS

Eltham was my home town for many years, therefore the local tramways hold a particular fascination for me. This passion has its beginnings in childhood memories of the sights and sounds of trams rumbling along Well Hall Road past our stop at the Welcome Inn. Attention has already been paid to the Woolwich area in three previous Middleton Press volumes: *Greenwich and Dartford Tramways*, *North Kent Tramways* and *Woolwich and Dartford Trolleybuses*. However, a recent influx of previously unpublished material, plus an increasing popular demand for more information have resulted in this new book.

I have called upon the resources of the following photographers and postcard collectors: G.F.Ashwell, A.H.Barkway, J.M.B.Bonell, C.Carter, Dr. Edwin Course, B.J.Cross, John Gent, George Gundry, Dave Jones, John Meredith, John Price, H.B.Priestley, D.Trevor Rowe, Geoffrey Southerden, Don Thompson, John Wills, and Richard Wiseman. My special thanks go to Ann Watkins for permission to use the views of the late Alan Watkins. Expert preparation of prints has again been in the capable hands of Stan Letts. I am also indebted to Mrs S.Leitch for the photographs taken by her late father, Dr. Hugh Nicol. The comprehensive photographic work of John Gillham has again added depth to the coverage of local streets.

My researches have been helped over the years by the staff at the Greenwich Local History Centre. Permission to use certain London Transport material has been granted by the LT Museum, Covent Garden, where there also exists a fine archive for the tramway student. Another seat of learning is the library of the National Tramway Museum, Crich, and I am very grateful to Rosy Thacker for all her assistance in locating articles from contemporary trade journals. I have consulted books on local history published by the Eltham Society and the exhaustive two volume work on the LCC tramways by E.R.Oakley. Moving images of the Eltham and Woolwich lines are readily available from Online in the second part of their London Trams video.

Finally, the tramway world is the poorer for the passing of Richard Elliott (1910-1995) who spent most of his career at Charlton Central Repair Depot. Several of Richard's views have been included in this album.

GEOGRAPHICAL SETTING

Woolwich is situated on the banks of the River Thames. The road south climbs out of the river valley to reach Eltham. Most of the undulating land hereabouts was once rich Kentish farmland, but urbanisation in the first decades of the twentieth century has altered the face of the landscape. However, ancient woodlands are still to be found on the slopes of Shooters Hill.

The two Metropolitan Boroughs of Woolwich and Greenwich were amalgamated to form the new London Borough of Greenwich in 1965.

Track map showing local tramways at their fullest extent.

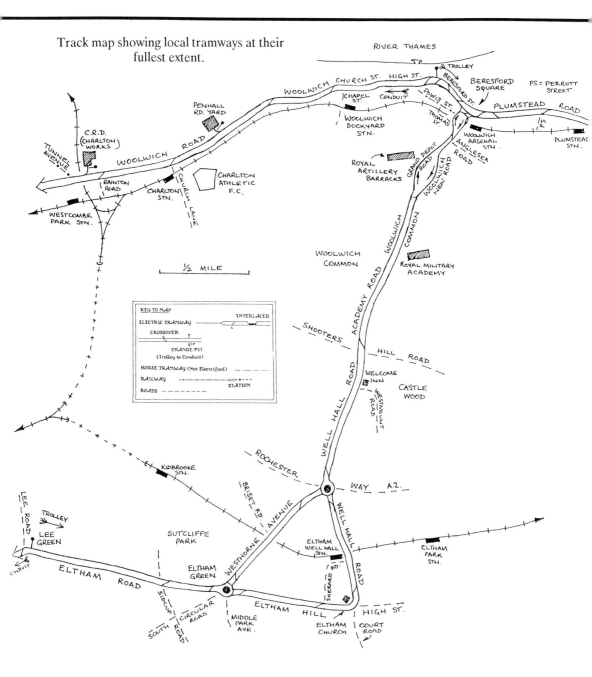

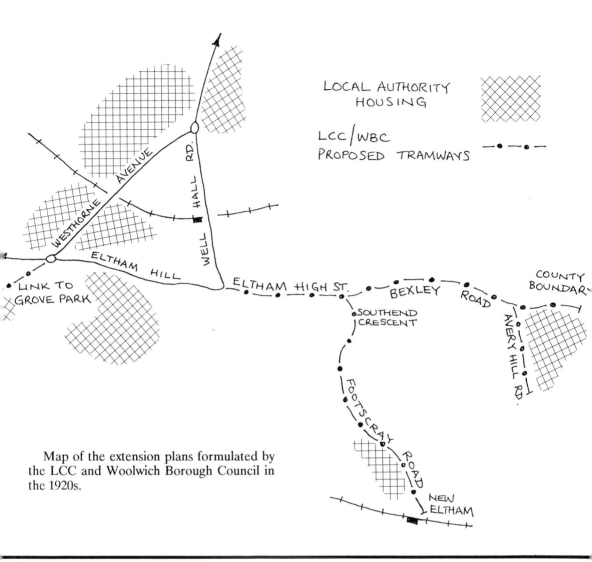

LOCAL AUTHORITY
HOUSING

LCC/WBC
PROPOSED TRAMWAYS

Map of the extension plans formulated by the LCC and Woolwich Borough Council in the 1920s.

HISTORICAL BACKGROUND

The streets of Woolwich first echoed to the sounds of horse trams in 1882 when the narrow gauge (3ft. 6ins./1067mm) rails of the Woolwich and South East London Tramways Company opened for traffic from Greenwich to Plumstead. This line was subsequently acquired by the London County Council with a view to conversion to electric operation. The LCC adopted the conduit system of electrification which was considerably more expens-ive than the conventional overhead wire method of current collection. The lifting of the horse car tracks and their replacement by standard gauge (4ft. 8½ins./1435mm) permanent way took longer than expected. Progress from Greenwich through Charlton to Woolwich was painfully slow, and as E.R.Oakley has noted in his splendid history of the LCC tramways, it took the council 8 years 5 months to reconstruct just over six miles of tramway! The conduit equipped lines to Woolwich Ferry opened on 5th April 1914. Here a change pit was built so that cars could proceed using their trolley poles on the overhead wires which were installed in the direction of Beresford Square and Abbey Wood. A better start was made to the east of town and the section from Abbey Wood to Beresford Square opened in April 1908.

A large central repair depot was constructed north of Woolwich Road, Charlton in 1908/9 to cater for the needs of the growing LCC system. A further route was inaugurated on 23rd July 1910 when a double track link through open country to Eltham brought the smart, new M class electric trams to a terminus on the corner of Well Hall Road and Eltham High Street. In order to placate the authorities at the Royal Greenwich Observatory, the Eltham service was equipped with double trolley wires so that no stray electric currents would be returned through the track to affect the delicate instruments at the observatory.

Throughout the First World War (1914-18) the local tramways performed sterling service transporting workers to the Woolwich Arsenal and catering for the needs of the many military establishments in the area. On the return of peace the progressive LCC continued to subscribe to an expansionist tramway philosophy. New lines were opened from Lee Green to Eltham Road, Lyme Farm on 29th November 1920 to be followed by the connection to the existing service 44 on 22nd March 1921.

Local services in May 1922:

36   Abbey Wood to Victoria Embankment,
      via Blackfriars Bridge.
38   Abbey Wood to Victoria Embankment,
      via Westminster Bridge.
40   Abbey Wood to Savoy Street, Strand,
      via Camberwell Green.
44   Beresford Square, Woolwich to Eltham.
46   Beresford Square, Woolwich to
      Southwark Bridge.

The above pattern of services was to last almost intact until the end of London's tramways.

In the 1920s new tramways were being promoted as an important adjunct to the post war housing estates being planned in the Eltham area. Although much road widening was undertaken by Woolwich Borough Council, many of the planned lines never left the drawing board. On a brighter note, construction started in November 1929 on the Westhorne Avenue extension. This line was opened from Well Hall Circus to Briset Road on 1st October 1931, and the southern portion to connect with service 46 at Eltham Green was inaugurated for traffic on 30th June 1932. Service 72 was diverted to run from Victoria Embankment via Westhorne Avenue to Beresford Square. The LCC had further powers to link up with the tracks at Grove Park, but before they could implement these, control over all London's tramways passed to the London Passenger Transport Board. This new organisation effectively sounded the death knell for the tramcar and any thoughts of new routes were quietly shelved.

The active dismantling of the London tramway system began in 1934, and by the end of the following year trolleybuses on routes 696 and 698 had invaded Woolwich as replacement for the Bexley, Erith and Dartford fleets. The trolleybus conversion programme was curtailed by the Second World War and the trams in Woolwich and Eltham were again called upon to provide much needed transport for munitions workers. After hostilities ended in 1945 the system enjoyed a too brief Indian summer which even included new trackwork for the Festival of Britain in 1951. Services 36,38,40,44,46 and 72 were fated to be the last in the capital to be converted to motor buses. On the last day, Saturday, 5th July 1952, business was brisk and in the early hours of Sunday, 6th July, car 187 battled its way from Woolwich to Eltham and thence to New Cross Depot to close the era of London's first generation tramway system.

Here matters rested for many years. The replacing diesel buses were gradually joined throughout the 1950s and 1960s by vast numbers of private cars and heavy goods vehicles, all of which contributed to the traffic nightmare of the metropolis. In the early 1990s plans were formulated for a return to modern tramways in the Croydon area, and as I write these notes, construction is about to start. One can only hope that it will not be too long before frequent, safe, comfortable and environmentally friendly light rail vehicles once again grace the streets of Woolwich, bringing all the benefits to the locality of an efficient and up to date transport system.

LEE GREEN TO
WESTHORNE AVENUE

1.   The tram is wilfully disobeying the *KEEP LEFT* bollard as it slows for the junction of Lee High Road and Burnt Ash Road. There was a considerable overlap of overhead wires above the conduit tracks at this location and this made it possible for trams using either method of current collection to reverse at the crossover in the foreground. The well stocked showroom of Lee Green Motors is an indicator of the coming affluence of the 1950s.   (J.C.Gillham)

2.   It is 25th April 1907 and the Burnt Ash Farm milk delivery cart has been somewhat delayed by swarms of temporary tramway enthusiasts out to inspect the new wonder of the age. Obviously from the look of the crowd this was basically "men's" work! Although many women would also avail themselves of the cheap fares and frequent services to go on shopping expeditions and trips to London. (J.H.Price Coll.)

3.   Car 1532 waits to nip across the junction into Eltham Road. Note the three disused indicator lamps above the destination box of this tram. The Lee Green to London service once showed the coloured lights BLUE-BLANK-BLUE, before the general introduction of service numbers from the summer of 1912.   (A.J.Watkins)

4. The Tilling Stevens petrol electric bus on route 21A tries to poach passengers from the 46 tram. In the background at Lee Green change pit two LCC cars stand at the end of the double trolley section to Eltham and Woolwich. The date is sometime between November 1920 when the track was extended along Eltham Road, and 13th November 1927 when the double overhead was converted to conventional single wire. (J.B.Gent Coll.)

5. In a few hours tramway activity will have ceased. Here on the very last day of London's trams, we observe cars 1906, 1862 and 1970. The nearer vehicle is in the process of "shooting" or expelling its plough so that it can continue towards Eltham whilst taking power from the overhead wire. (J.H.Meredith)

6. Here we have a good general view of Lee Green change pit. The canvas hut on the extreme right of the picture afforded the attendant some protection from the elements. In the centre of the view a plough fork is positioned ready for the next city bound car. Finally, this June 1952 scene depicts a row of small shops which would become prime candidates for demolition in the "knock 'em down and rebuilt 'em ugly" supermarket revolution of the 1960s. (J.C.Gillham)

Lee Green 1910.

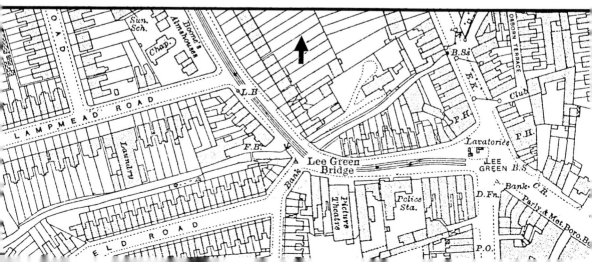

7. With a skill born of experience, the change pit attendant gently guides the plough into the carrier fixed under the tramcar on the left. In the foreground we note that the conduit slot rails are badly worn. This is due in part to the unique nature of the Lee Green operation where eastbound cars accelerated past the change pit to eject the plough with some speed. The usual London routine at other locations where trams changed from the conduit to the overhead involved a compulsory stop where passengers boarded and alighted.
(J.C.Gillham)

8. We now pass into the leafy suburbs. At the corner of Leyland Road and Eltham Road only a single motorist intrudes on the London Transport presence of a tower wagon and a distant tramcar. (A.J.Watkins)

9. Former West Ham car 334 does not have to display the red and white LAST TRAM WEEK poster as its advert mouldings are narrowly spaced. A shaft of sunlight catches the new bus stop which will be unveiled in a few days time for passengers on new routes 182 and 186. (R.J.S.Wiseman)

10. On a warm summer's day long ago a tram
pauses by the entrance to Hornpark Lane. The
two lines of trees obscure the rather substantial
detached houses set back from Eltham Road.
Many of the local residents objected to the
building of this tramway, because in the words
of one worthy.."the tramcars would encourage
the cheaper element of society to commit a
nuisance outside our properties.."
(A.J.Watkins)

11. TRACK UP signs at the junction of Sidcup Road act as a warning to other traffic, whilst LT rather begrudgingly relays track which will be abandoned well before it is life expired. Roadworks at this location in 1974 revealed several lengths of girder rail and the author was instrumental in saving a section. A shim of this rail forms part of the Tramway and Light Railway Society (Sussex area) trophy presented each year for the best model tramcar. (A.J.Watkins)

Extract from LT circular February 1936.

882.—ELTHAM ROAD, LEE—SERVICE Nos. 46, 72.

Drivers are reminded that under the Ministry of Transport Regulation the speed of cars when crossing the junction of the Sidcup by-pass and Eltham Road must not exceed **10 miles an hour.**

12. At Eltham Green by the southern boundary of Sutcliffe Park service 44 terminated on a crossover outside the Yorkshire Grey public house. The 44s were extended here on 5th May 1948 to lift some of the pressure from the Central Bus department, where an acute post war vehicle shortage had affected the parallel bus route. Note that LT was nothing but lavish with its stop "flags"; one wonders whether the tram, bus and Green Line coach stops could have been combined in one display on a single post! (J.C.Gillham)

Extract from LT timetable December 1943.

ROUTE 44 | **Woolwich - Eltham** | P.M. times are in heavy figures

Via New Road, (return via Grand Depot Road), Woolwich Common, Academy Road, Well Hall Road.
RAILWAY STATIONS SERVED : Woolwich Arsenal, Eltham Well Hall.
Service interval : WEEKDAYS ONLY, 8 minutes (Saturday afternoon 5 minutes, evenings 12 minutes.).

WEEKDAYS	First			Last ¶				WEEKDAYS	First		Last ¶		
WOOLWICH *Beresford Square*	6 3	6 10	..	9 14	10 28	..	...	ELTHAM *Church*	..	6 32	..	9 35	10 49
Dickson Road *Well Hall Road*	6 15	6 22	..	9 26	10 40	..	..	Dickson Road *Well Hall Road*..	6 17	6 39	..	9 42	10 56
ELTHAM *Church*	..	6 29	..	9 33	10 47	..	..	WOOLWICH *Beresford Square*	6 29	6 51	..	9 54	11 8

¶–Special late journey.

ROUTE 46 | **Woolwich - Eltham - Lewisham - New Cross - Southwark** | P.M. times are in heavy figures

Via New Rd. (return via Grand Depot Rd.), Woolwich Common, Academy Rd., Well Hall Rd.. Eltham Hill. Eltham Rd., Lee Green, Lee High Rd., Loampit Vale, Loampit Hill, Lewisham Way, New Cross Rd., Old Kent Rd., Great Dover Street, Marshalsea Rd., Southwark Bridge Rd., Southwark Bridge
RAILWAY STATIONS SERVED : Woolwich Arsenal, Eltham Well Hall, Lewisham, St. Johns, New Cross Gate, Borough.
Service interval : Woolwich–New Cross, MONDAY to FRIDAY 6 minutes (peak hours 3 minutes, evening 12 minutes), SATURDAY 6 minutes (peak hours 3 minutes, afternoon 5 minutes, evening 12 minutes), SUNDAY 10 minutes (evening 12 minutes). New Cross–City, WEEKDAYS 6 minutes (evening 12 minutes), SUNDAY 10 minutes (evening 12 minutes).

	WEEKDAYS First			MONDAY to FRIDAY Last			SATURDAY Last			SUNDAY First				SUNDAY Last		
WOOLWICH *Beresford Square*	....	4 33	4 34	5 7	...	8 48	10 25	10 31	...	4 43	5 2	5 36	7 6	8 48	10 20	10 31
Dickson Road *Well Hall Road*	...	4 45	4 46	5 19	..	9 0	10 32	10 43	...	4 54	5 14	5 48	7 18	9 0	10 32	10 43
Eltham *Church*	4 0	4 52	4 53	5 26	..	9 7	10 39	10 50	...	5 0	5 21	5 55	7 25	9 7	10 39	10 50
Lee Green *Tigers Head*	4 8	..	5 1	5 34	..	9 15	10 47	..	...	..	5 29	6 3	7 33	9 15	10 47	
Lewisham *Obelisk*	4 15	..	5 9	5 42	..	9 23	10 55	..	...	..	6 11	7 41	9 23	10 55		
New Cross Gate	4 25	5 10	..	5 20	5 53	..	9 34	11 6	..	...	..	6 22	7 51	9 34	11 6	
CITY *Southwark*	4 46	5 32	..	6 15	..	9 56	..	9 56	..	...	8 11	9 56				

	WEEKDAYS First			MONDAY to FRIDAY Last			SATURDAY Last		SUNDAY First				SUNDAY Last	
CITY *Southwark*	..	..	4 50	5 34	..	10 0	..	..	..	..	8 16	10 0	..
New Cross Gate	3 31	3 39	5 1	5 12	5 56	10 22	10 34	10 22	10 34	..	5 27	8 36	10 22	10 34
Lewisham *Obelisk*	3 42	3 50	5 12	5 23	6 7	10 33	10 45	10 33	10 45	..	5 38	8 46	10 33	10 45
Lee Green *Tigers Head*	3 50	3 58	5 20	5 31	6 15	10 41	10 53	10 41	10 53	5 31	5 46	8 53	10 41	10 53
Eltham *Church*	3 58	4 6	4 54	5 28	5 39	6 23	10 49	11 1	10 49	11 1	5 2	5 39	5 54	9 0	10 49	11 1
Dickson Road *Well Hall Road*	..	4 13	5 1	5 35	5 46	6 20	10 56	11 8	10 56	11 8	5 9	5 46	6 1	9 6	10 56	11 8
WOOLWICH *Beresford Square*	..	4 25	5 13	5 47	5 58	6 42	11 8	11 20	11 8	11 20	5 21	5 58	6 13	9 17	11 8	11 20

*–Special early journey.

13. Those were the days when everyone took the tramcar! With cheap fares and a very frequent service, it is no surprise that car 1929 is full. This is a classic broadside view of a tram as it rests in the sunshine at Eltham Green. At the motorman's end an inspector stands in the shadows. (J.C.Gillham)

14. Our vantage point now changes to the top deck of an Eltham bound car. Going in the opposite direction is car 1910, probably on its very last passenger journey to New Cross Depot. The chalk messages on the dash indicate that this is the last day, 5th July 1952. (C.Carter)

15. Almost out of camera shot is the inspector's cabin, which is the nerve centre of tramway control here at the Yorkshire Grey roundabout. Car 312 displays the destination MIDDLE PARK AVENUE. This was considered more in keeping with the temperance traditions of the former LCC tramways, where the idea of calling the terminus after the nearby hostelry would have fallen on stony ground! (J.C.Gillham)

16. The driver of this service 72 car has obviously experienced some difficulty with the automatic points leading to Westhorne Avenue. He gingerly backs the tram up before returning to the other end of the car to make a fresh attempt. Kerb stones are stacked at the side of the road in readiness for the rebuilding of the junction as a roundabout. (H.Nicol)

17. The relocation of tracks at the Yorkshire Grey roundabout occurred in the summer of 1935; the completed layout was used by trams on 25th August that year. Car 837 has just disturbed the permanent way department hard at work installing the crossover opposite Eltham Green Road. The brand new LT passenger shelter has yet to be delivered. (G.N.Southerden)

731.—SERVICES 46 & 72—AUTOMATIC POINTS.

Notice to Motormen—Westhorne Avenue Circus.

The electrically operated point has been removed from the existing position at the junction of Eltham Road and Westhorne Avenue, and is now situated at the Circus at the junction with Westhorne Avenue, and is controlled by a skate on Pole No. 51.

Cars for Westhorne Avenue pass under the skate with power " ON."

Cars for Eltham Church pass under the skate with power " OFF."

Cars from Westhorne Avenue to London will automatically operate the points at the junction of the Circus and Eltham Road when they pass under the skate at Pole No. 64, whether power is " ON " or " OFF."

Cars from London to Eltham Church will automatically operate the points at the junction of the Circus and Eltham Road when they pass under the skate at Pole No. 64, whether power is " ON " or " OFF."

The Signal on Pole No. 50 indicates the position of the electrically operated Frog at Pole No. 51, and shows the Motormen whether the Frog has been operated for the route they should take. Motormen must observe that the points have been correctly operated.

The speed of cars is Not to exceed four miles per hour when passing under the skates.

Extract from LT circular September 1935.

18. On the north side of the roundabout car 1862 sails along with its cargo of last day trippers. This vehicle belongs to the HR2 class, more often associated with the Dulwich services featured in companion album *Camberwell and West Norwood Tramways.* As the London system contracted, so the best cars found themselves allocated to the two last depots - Abbey Wood and New Cross. (J.C.Gillham)

19. Pride of place in this view belongs to the Woolwich Borough Council cart placed next to the new curve by the southern extension of Westhorne Avenue. This road was meant to carry connecting lines to Grove Park, but the arrival of LT in 1933 put paid to the project. Note the rather stylish white house on the corner of Middle Park Avenue. (H.Nicol)

20. The Yorkshire Grey can be glimpsed behind the 72 tram turning into Westhorne Avenue. Note that new traction standards are being positioned. (H.Nicol)

21. The photographer is standing on the Woolwich bound track in Westhorne Avenue. The landscape behind the tram will not retain its rural aspect for much longer, and soon a mixture of local authority and private housing will oust the fields and hedgerows. (H.Nicol)

22. Construction of the roundabout is almost complete as car 962 halts at the stop at the foot of Westhorne Avenue. In the distance the wooded slopes of Shooters Hill offer a welcome change from the encroaching suburbia. (G.N.Southerden)

23. This view was taken a week before final abandonment and the scene has little altered since pre-war days. Westhorne Avenue was later rebuilt as a dual carriageway after removal of the rails and traction standards. Strangely enough, this wholesale destruction omitted the section box on the left of the picture and it survived into the 1960s. (J.C.Gillham)

24. Tramlines form a neat symmetry; the facing points are set for Eltham Hill. In May 1952 it was perfectly possible to stand in the middle of the carriageway to take this shot. In the 1990s the constant stream of traffic on the South Circular Road would make a photo from this location well nigh impossible. (J.C.Gillham)

Extract from LT circular December 1935.

807.—ELTHAM ROAD ROUNDABOUT.

Notice to Motormen—Service Nos. 44, 46 and 72.

The following regulation of the Ministry of Transport must be strictly observed :—

Speed.—The speed of cars must not exceed 5 m.p.h. through all junctions, and round curves of less than 75 ft radius.

25. A spot of bother delays car 1825 on 6th October 1951. The points here had a reputation for having a mind of their own, and it was not an uncommon sight to observe the emergency crew in attendance trying to sort out the point motors. Here it seems that the job has been completed and final checks are made before the two LT workmen can go off to the next problem. (J.M.B.Bonell)

Extract from LT timetable December 1943.

ROUTE **72**	**Woolwich - Lewisham - Camberwell - Savoy Street**	P.M. times are in heavy figures

Via New Road, (return via Grand Depot Road), Woolwich Common, Academy Road, Well Hall Road, Westhorne Avenue, Eltham Road, Lee Green, Lee High Road, Loampit Vale, Loampit Hill, Lewisham Way, New Cross Road, Queens Road, Peckham H gh Street, Peckham Road, Camberwell Church Street, Camberwell New Road, Kennington Park Road, Kennington Road, Westminster Bridge Road, Westminster Bridge, Victoria Embankment.

RAILWAY STATIONS SERVED : Woolwich Arsenal, Lewisham, St. Johns, New Cross Gate, Queens Road, Oval, Lambeth North, Westminster, Charing Cross.

Service interval : WEEKDAYS, 8 mins. (evening 12 mins.), SUNDAY, morning and evening 12 mins., afternoon 10 mins.

	WEEKDAYS						SUNDAY			WEEKDAYS						SUNDAY	
	First			Last			First	Last			First			Last			First	Last
	*X	X			SO	MF				X					SO	MF		
WOOLWICH *Beresford Square*	5 34	6 14	....	6 28	8 58	9 11	10 45	9 2	10 45	VICTORIA EMB. *Savoy St*	..	..	7 39	9 24	10 15	10 30	....	....
Eltham *Middle Park Avenue* ...	5 50	6 30	..	6 44	9 14	9 27	11 1	9 19	11 1	Kennington Gate	..	..	7 52	9 39	10 30	10 45	..	..
Lewisham *Obelisk*				6 58	9 28	9 41	11 15	9 31	11 15	Camberwell Green	..	..	7 58	9 46	10 37	10 52	..	..
New Cross Gate	..	..	7 2	7 9	9 39	9 52	11 26	9 41	11 26	New Cross Gate	4 49	5 44	8 9	9 59	10 50	11 5	8 19	9 53
Camberwell Green			7 15	7 22	9 52	10 5	....	....	....	Lewisham *Obelisk*	5 0	5 55	8 19	10 10	....	..	8 29	10 4
Kennington Gate			7 22	7 29	9 59	10 12	..	..	..	Eltham *Well Hall Circus* ..	5 17	6 12	8 35	10 27	..	..	8 45	10 21
VICTORIA EMBANK. *Savoy St.*			7 37	7 44	10 14	10 27	....	....	....	WOOLWICH *Beresford Sq.*	5 30	6 25	8 48	10 40	....	..	8 58	10 34

MF—Monday to Friday only. SO—Saturday only. *—Special early journey. X—Extra Car.

SPECIAL EARLY MORNING JOURNEYS—SUNDAY

Wickham Lane to Greenwich *South Street* at 6 32, 7 23 a.m.
Wickham Lane to New Cross Gate at 7 39, 8 27 a.m.
New Cross Gate to Kennington Gate at 5 57 a.m.
New Cross Gate to Wickham Lane at 5 48 a.m.
Kennington Gate to Wickham Lane at 6 19 a.m.
Greenwich *South Street* to Wickham Lane at 7 5, 7 55 a.m.

26. The black and white fencing encircling the roudabout was a relic of the wartime blackout regulations. In peak periods the number of trams passing this junction every hour was just under sixty. (R.J.Harley Coll.)

27. Car 1363 is in sparkling condition as it waits at the foot of Westhorne Avenue whilst the official inspection takes place. The date is 29th June 1932. This was the high watermark of the LCC tramways, a year later the system would be in the hands of new owners who had a totally different transport policy. (H.Nicol)

28. This is the first of three previously unpublished views of the construction of the Westhorne Avenue tramway. Lines were laid as a conventional street tramway, and the opportunity to use reserved track in the middle of a dual carriageway road was not taken. The most likely explanation for this layout lies with Woolwich Borough Council who asked the LCC to install the "tried and tested" street track rather than anything "fancy". (H.Nicol)

29. Work is interrupted for Dr.Nicol to record the scene near the corner of Pinnell Road. The team of men in the centre is grappling with a heavy length of girder rail. This will be positioned on temporary wedges before tie bars, similar to those in the foreground, are screwed in place to keep the rails to gauge. (H.Nicol)

RAIL SECTIONS

British Standard Sections.—The section of tramway rail adopted in Great Britain is the grooved girder rail shown in Fig. 2, where a is the flange, b the web, c the tread, d the check, and e the groove. Five different sections of this have been standardized by the Engineering Standards Committee for straight-line work, and five for curve work, the latter varying from the former in the width and depth of the groove. For straight-line work the groove is $1\frac{1}{8}$ inches wide by $1\frac{1}{8}$ inches deep, and for curve work $1\frac{1}{4}$ inches wide and $1\frac{1}{4}$ inches deep. The various sections are known as British Standard No. 1, No. 2, etc., usually abbreviated to B.S. No. 1, etc., the curve sections having the letter c after the number. The weights of the various sections, with the depths of the sections and the widths of the flanges, are given in Table II.

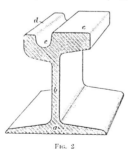

FIG. 2

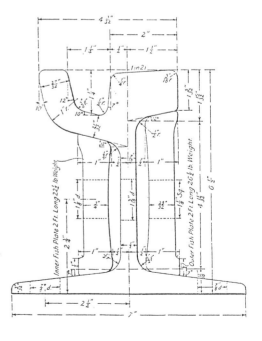

TABLE II

STANDARD TRAMWAY-RAIL SECTIONS AND WEIGHTS

British Standard Rail Section Number	Weight Pounds Per Yard	Depth of Section Inches	Width of Flange Inches	British Standard Rail Section Number	Weight Pounds Per Yard	Depth of Section Inches	Width of Flange Inches
1	90	$6\frac{1}{4}$	$6\frac{1}{2}$	3c	106	$6\frac{1}{2}$	7
1c	96	$6\frac{1}{4}$	$6\frac{1}{2}$	4	105	7	7
2	95	$6\frac{1}{4}$	7	4c	111	7	7
2c	101	$6\frac{1}{4}$	7	5	110	7	7
3	100	$6\frac{1}{2}$	7	5c	116	7	7

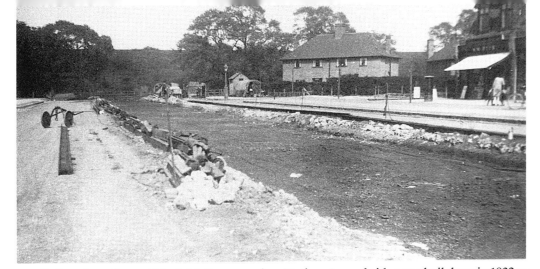

30. Before the rails could be laid, the ground had to be prepared as is seen in this photo. In the background is the embankment of the railway line leading to Eltham Well Hall Station. A new bridge was built here in 1932 so that the two halves of Westhorne Avenue could be linked. (H.Nicol)

31. Even in 1952 there was still very little traffic on this road, which makes it perfectly safe for car 1908 to halt for a photo stop on the last day of London's tramways. This scene has altered considerably in the intervening years and this location now features a flyover and interchange with the Rochester Way Relief Road. (J.H.Meredith)

32. On 2nd June 1951 car 305 is pictured on the northern section of Westhorne Avenue. This tram is working off route on a special service 44 to Eltham Green. This recalls the arrangement from 1st October 1931 to 30th June 1932 when cars on service 44 temporarily worked this stretch before the introduction of the through service 72. (E.Course)

ELTHAM HILL TO ELTHAM CHURCH

33. We now begin our gentle ascent to St.John's Church, Eltham High Street. The two trams in this view are both refugees from the East End: on the left an ex West Ham car and on the right a vehicle formerly owned by East Ham Corporation. These cars came south of the river to Abbey Wood Depot as a result of trolleybus coversions in their native territory. (J.C.Gillham)

34. Car 1497 is pictured in pre war, unvestibuled state as it descends Eltham Hill. Construction of housing in Green Way is still proceeding in this view dated 22nd October 1936. (H.F.Wheeller/R.S.Carpenter Coll.)

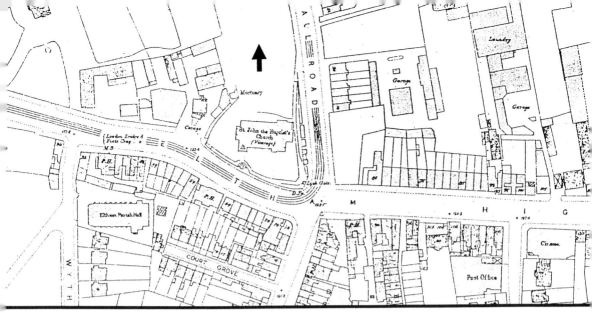

Eltham Town Centre 1937.

35. Eltham Swimming Baths opened on 4th April 1939 and patrons alighted from their trams at the two stops in this picture. The tram in the middle distance obscures the entrance to Sherard Road where the residents had a bitter fight with London Transport to stop the proposed installation of a trolleybus turning loop. In the event all the legal action was meaningless as the war intervened and the trams were later replaced by diesel buses. (R.J.S.Wiseman)

36. Cars 1861 and 93 pass between the National Provincial Bank and the War Memorial on Eltham High Street. At the unveiling ceremony of the memorial in 1924, as a mark of respect, the tram service outside was halted and worked in two sections so that the many relatives of those fallen in the First World War could assemble on the roadway. (J.H.Meredith)

Au 8925
200 L.T. Trams

T	Cge Bricklayers Arms Tower Bridge	44
E	Cge New X Gate, or Marquis Elephant of Kennington Gt	46
R	Cge Clock Tr, Lewisham Rye Lane	3d
Q	Queens Road Station	Sgle

3		17
4		16
6d		15
7		14
8		13
9		12
10		11

Issued subject to the bye-laws, conditions and regulations of the Board in force at time of issue

---

Fc 3052
20J London Transport Trams

Ch	Bricklayers Arms Tower Bridge	44
V	New X Gt or Marquis Vict Embankmt, Savoy St or Regency Street	46
Ch	Clock Tr, Lewisham Camberwell Green	4d
R	Rye Lane	Single

3		15
4		14
5		13
7		12
8		11
9		10

Issued subject to the bye-laws, conditions and regulations of the Board in force at the time of issue. Available on day of issue only to point indicated by the punch hole and must be shown or given up on demand.

Do 3907
B L.T. Trams & Trolleybuses

1		21
1a		20
2		19
2a		18
3		17
4		16
5		15
6		14
6a		13
7		12
8		11
9		10

S For conditions see back

1¼d 2d
1d Child

37. You can almost hear the growl of the motors and the screech of the wheels as this tram grinds round the corner from Eltham High Street into Well Hall Road. On the right is the boundary wall of St.John's Church; historical records note that the first vicar of Eltham was Adam de Bromleigh in 1160. (D.Trevor Rowe)

→

38. Electric versus Diesel! The two rivals prepare to leave Well Hall Road in opposite directions. The RTL type bus on route 21 demonstrates the early post war restricted destination display as well as the distinctive cream painted upper deck window surrounds which were later to receive the standard LT red. The sharp bend which the tram is about to negotiate was one of the reasons why the long Feltham type cars were not allowed on the Eltham routes. On the extreme left of the picture is the former LCC passenger shelter, which still exists today. It was connected to the LT internal telephone system and was listed under the numbers OT126 and 654 in the official timetable. (A.J.Watkins)

Extract from LT circular August 1934.

335.—JUNCTION OF ELTHAM HIGH STREET WITH COURT YARD AND WELL HALL ROAD.

In Well Hall Road.

Proceeding to Woolwich.

Tramcars to make a tail stop at tramway standard No. 293, as at present.

Proceeding to London.

Tramcars to make a tail stop at tramway standard No. 294, as at present.

In Court Yard.

Proceeding to Eltham.

Omnibuses to stop outside Nos. 14/16, Court Yard, as at present.

Proceeding to Beckenham.

Omnibuses to stop outside " The Crown " P.H., as at present.

In Eltham High Street.

Proceeding Eastward.

Omnibuses to make a tail stop at the party-wall of Nos. 73/75.

Proceeding Westward.

Omnibuses to stop outside No. 90, as at present.

39. A crew member switches the points as car 304 prepares to reverse on the facing crossover at Eltham Church. This was the original 1910 terminus and it remained in regular use for service 44 until 5th May 1948. Even so, after this date there were still occasional short workings as seen here on 10th May 1952. (J.C.Gillham)

40. We look in the other direction to the previous view in time to catch car 336 which is creeping forward in response to the "OK" from the chap pushing the point lever. (C.Carter)

41. The single deck bus behind car 332 is on its way to the Kentish suburbs. Nowadays this view could be repeated - except for the bus and tram - as the parade of shops in the background has hardly altered. However, the modern curse of queuing motor traffic is now almost a permanent fixture at this road junction. (J.C.Gillham)

42. Towards the end of the tramway era it became more hazardous to step out into the roadway to catch the tram. Of course, LT wanted to phase out this form of transport as soon as possible, so they had no interest in providing extra passenger loading islands. People boarding car 82 at least had the conductor on the rear platform to help them up on to the vehicle. (J.Wills)

43. The undulating nature of the local landscape is apparent in this view looking down Well Hall Road to the station bridge. Car 1248 climbs the gradient. This car was reconditioned by LT in January 1936 and was finally withdrawn from New Cross Depot in April 1951. A full description of this class can be found in *Lewisham and Catford Tramways*. (A.J.Watkins)

44. Well Hall Road was extended from the railway bridge to St.John's Church in 1905. The trams arrived five years later, not long before this photo was taken with an LCC M class four wheel car passing in front of Spencer Gardens. Notice that the eastern side of Well Hall Road has yet to be developed. (G.L.Gundry Coll.)

45. Two trams and a taxi face the amber light at the corner of Sherard Road and Glenlea Road. The blue TRAM STOP, REQUEST will shortly be replaced by the red version employed by the central bus department. (R.J.S.Wiseman)

46. Scenes such as this one at Eltham Well Hall Station now seem an age away, especially when one takes into account the changes since this view was taken. The Rochester Way Relief Road now dives under this spot, Well Hall Station has been closed, the 1952 bus station off Sherard Road has disappeared into the hole which is now the motorway, and finally, a new bus and rail interchange has been built to the right of the picture. (A.J.Watkins)

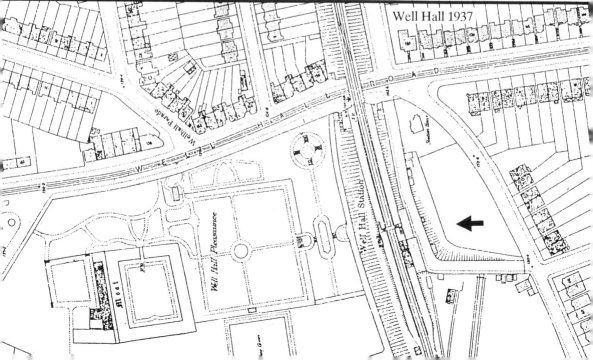

47. We look out from the platform at Well Hall Station towards Fysons Bakery at the corner of Dunvegan Road. Many of the streets on the Corbett estate which was developed between 1900 and 1914, bear Scottish names. Just to the right of the oncoming tramcar is the entrance to Craigton Road, boyhood home of Bob Hope who later found fame and fortune in Hollywood. (E.Course)

48. A quiet winter Sunday sees car 93 passing a shuttered Royal Arsenal Cooperative Society store at Well Hall. This building was constructed in 1906 and demolished in 1964 to make way for a supermarket. On the opposite side of the road are the ornamental gardens of Well Hall Pleasaunce laid out on the site of Well Hall House, home of the writer Edith Nesbit from 1899 to 1922. Miss Nesbit was a well known local figure and often she would venture out with a jug of tea to sustain passing tram crews. (A.J.Watkins)

49. We now approach the roundabout referred to as Well Hall Circus in official LT timetables. The date is 29th December 1948 and the tram on which we are travelling slows for the points on the pedestrian crossing which has yet to receive its zebra stripes. (H.B.Priestley)

50. In the foreground we note some basic maintenance to the points which are set on this occasion for cars on services 44 and 46. Note in those days there were no warning cones for roadworks, one assumes that if a motorist drove into the hole, it would be deemed his own fault for not looking where he was going! In the background is the splendid 1936 Odeon cinema which was modernised in the multi-screen revolution of the 1970s. (A.J.Watkins)

51. The automatic points have failed again, obliging the driver of car 1946 to do it the old fashioned way. This was a common occurrence in the twilight months of the system when the powers that be were loath to fork out money for repairs. A motorman told one enthusiast that the coils of the point motors had burnt out, and at £20 each it wasn't worth replacing them! (R.J.S.Wiseman)

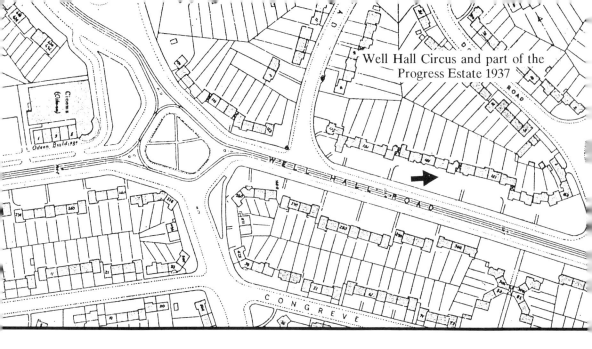

Well Hall Circus and part of the Progress Estate 1937

52. The fume ridden frenzy of the 1990s is well in the future as we admire this wonderful study of one of the domed roof, reconditioned cars as it negotiates Well Hall roundabout. The local council always paid attention to the floral arrangements on the green, so that a splash of colour added to the beauty of a fine summer's day. (R.J.Harley Coll.)

53. The lines from Westhorne Avenue rejoin those to Eltham Church at the south west corner of Well Hall Circus. A speeding tram has just passed the war damaged St.Barnabas Church. The building, to a design by Sir Gilbert Scott, dates from 1857 and was moved from Woolwich Dockyard to this location in 1933. (J.C.Gillham)

54. The roundabout at Well Hall was constructed in 1931 in association with works on the Westhorne Avenue extension. Here we look past Dickson Road crossover to the rising ground where the Welcome Inn is situated. (J.C.Gillham)

55. Early days on Well Hall Road shows that the local children had plenty of space to play. All they had to do was to get out of the way of the trams which plied the route every ten minutes. A ride from Woolwich to Eltham would have cost two old pence. (G.L.Gundry Coll.)

56. The rural aspect of Well Hall Road was transformed in 1915 when accommodation, both temporary and permanent, sprung up beside the tramway. Its purpose was to house the influx of manpower needed for the armaments industry in Woolwich Arsenal. Some of the Eltham hutments, cabins built as hostels for arms workers, are seen to left of car 1717. (G.L.Gundry Coll.)

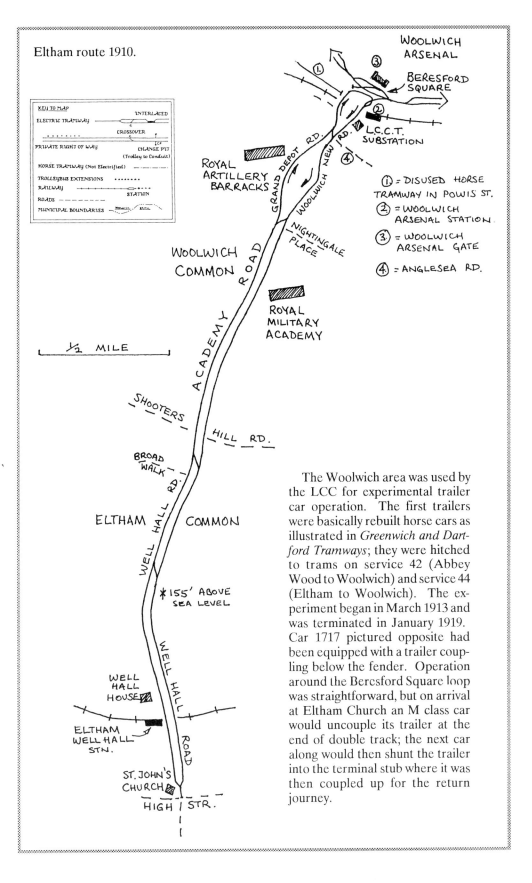

Eltham route 1910.

KEY TO MAP

ELECTRIC TRAMWAY —————— INTERLACED

CROSSOVER

PRIVATE RIGHT OF WAY · · · · · · · · · CHANGE PIT
(Trolley to Conduit)

HORSE TRAMWAY (Not Electrified) — · · — · · —

TROLLEYBUS EXTENSIONS · · · · · · · ·

RAILWAY ———————— STATION

ROADS — — — — — —

MUNICIPAL BOUNDARIES

WOOLWICH ARSENAL

BERESFORD SQUARE

L.C.C.T. SUBSTATION

① = DISUSED HORSE TRAMWAY IN POWIS ST.

② = WOOLWICH ARSENAL STATION.

③ = WOOLWICH ARSENAL GATE

④ = ANGLESEA RD.

ROYAL ARTILLERY BARRACKS

GRAND DEPOT RD.

WOOLWICH NEW RD.

NIGHTINGALE PLACE

WOOLWICH COMMON ROAD

ACADEMY ROAD

ROYAL MILITARY ACADEMY

½ MILE

SHOOTERS HILL RD.

BROAD WALK RD.

ELTHAM COMMON

WELL HALL RD.

✳ 155' ABOVE SEA LEVEL

WELL HALL ROAD

WELL HALL HOUSE

ELTHAM WELL HALL STN.

ST. JOHN'S CHURCH

HIGH STR.

The Woolwich area was used by the LCC for experimental trailer car operation. The first trailers were basically rebuilt horse cars as illustrated in *Greenwich and Dartford Tramways*; they were hitched to trams on service 42 (Abbey Wood to Woolwich) and service 44 (Eltham to Woolwich). The experiment began in March 1913 and was terminated in January 1919. Car 1717 pictured opposite had been equipped with a trailer coupling below the fender. Operation around the Beresford Square loop was straightforward, but on arrival at Eltham Church an M class car would uncouple its trailer at the end of double track; the next car along would then shunt the trailer into the terminal stub where it was then coupled up for the return journey.

57. Car 1718 heads for Eltham past some of the mature trees which marked the former field boundaries. The new housing is part of the Progress Estate constructed between February and December 1915. It is a prime example of "cottage style" and deservedly the whole estate has been designated a conservation area. (G.L.Gundry Coll.)

58. Temporary housing of another sort - the pre-fab - came to the area in the immediate post Second World War years. A couple of pre-fabs can be observed behind car 2003 as it crests the hill on Monday morning, 30th June 1952. (E.Course)

59. The author is now very much on home territory as he used to walk with his mother up the hill from his house in Mayday Gardens to catch the tram here at the Welcome Inn stop. On a fine June day in 1952 a well loaded 72 skips past Dunblane Road as the conductor looks up the stairs to see if any passengers want to alight. (J.C.Gillham)

60. Trouble ahead! The conductor peers out to ascertain the delay as the overhead tower wagon straddles the track. Hopefully, it will soon move over to let car 87 pass on its depot run back to Abbey Wood. (D.Jones Coll.)

61. Car 1177 has just passed the traffic lights at the junction with Shooters Hill Road and it now heads along Academy Road in the direction of Woolwich. This particular vehicle was reconditioned by LT in February 1936 and survived until January 1952. (C.Carter)

62. Right until the end of tramway operation the ride across Woolwich Common had a rustic quality which was enhanced by the tall elm trees and the swathes of grasses by the roadside. Here on the last day the messages from disgruntled enthusiasts reflect a distinct disenchantment with LT and a longing to return to the past glories of the LCC. (R.B.Parr/NTM)

Extract from LT circular April 1938.

1794.—ROYAL HERBERT HOSPITAL, WOOLWICH—VOUCHERS FOR TRAMWAY TRAVEL.

Notice to Conductors—New Cross, Abbey Wood, Camberwell, Hampstead and Holloway Depots.

Conductors are reminded of the arrangements made for the acceptance on trams of vouchers issued by the Royal Herbert Hospital, Woolwich, to patients for travel from the hospital in Shooters Hill Road to various railway stations. Particulars of the journeys are as follows :—

From Shooters Hill Road to	Change at	Services.	Single Fare. Ordinary	Single Fare. Mid-day.
			d.	d.
1. Waterloo Station	Tower Bridge Road	46 ; 68	5	2
2. Victoria	New Cross	72; 46 ; 54	5	2
3. London Bridge—				
Shooters Hill Road to Beresford Square ...	Direct	44 ; 46 ; 72	2	1
Beresford Square to London Bridge ...	Greenwich Church	36; 38; 40; 70	5	2
4. Westminster	New Cross	72; 46,35; 36; 38; 40 ; 66 ; 72	5	2
5. St. Pancras—				
Shooters Hill Road to Bloomsbury	New Cross	72; 46 ; 35	5	2
Bloomsbury to Holborn Hall	Direct	35	1	1
Holborn Hall to St. Pancras	Direct	3 ; 7	1	1

On presentation of a voucher the conductor must issue **in exchange therefor** the appropriate single fare ticket, direct or transfer according to the journey and value stated on the voucher.

Vouchers will be handed in with the day's takings and treated as cash.

63. With not a house in sight and very little competing traffic the tramride across the common could be brisk. However, on this day the service has suffered a temporary interruption as a tram slows for trackworks. The PW department's compressor is taking current from a pole clipped to the overhead wire.
(E.Course)

64. This view of car 1378 dates from the late 1920s. The tram is in its original LCC livery which by this time had weathered to a dull brown and cream. The service display EX denotes an extra vehicle employed to cater for traffic needs outside the normal timetable.
(A.H.Barkway)

65. At almost the same location as the previous view, but some twenty years and a world war later, this former East Ham car bears the standard LT livery of red and cream. The railings behind the tram enclose the grounds of the Royal Military Academy. (R.Elliott)

66. The overhead fittings show evidence of the double trolley system which breathed its last on 13th November 1927. The car in the picture is painted in the later LCC livery of crimson and cream. (A.H.Barkway)

ROUTE No. 34.

Woolwich Free Ferry to Abbey Wood, and Beresford Square to Eltham (Electric Traction), and Chapel Street to Woolwich Free Ferry (Horse Traction).

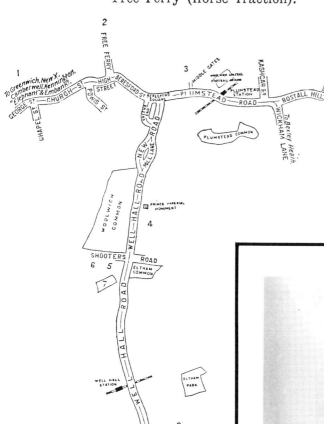

1. Woolwich Dockyard.
2. Woolwich Ferry.
3. Woolwich Arsenal.
4. Royal Military Academy.
5. Royal Herbert Hospital.
6. Brook Fever Hospital.
7. Greenwich Cemetery.
8. Eaglesfield.

Extract from LCC guide 1911.

67. Car 1436 in brand new condition passes along Woolwich Common towards the junction with Nightingale Place. Contemporary reports tell of the popularity of the tramway which served a natural traffic route. Before the introduction of the 44 service number in the summer of 1912 Eltham cars showed WHITE-BLANK-WHITE on the three coloured lights above the indicator blind. (R.J.Harley Coll.)

68. The photographer stands at the entrance to the delightfully named Ha-Ha Road as he points his camera at one of the series 552-601 cars (described fully in *Hampstead and Highgate Tramways*) loading in front of the Barrack Tavern. What followed after the trams were abandoned certainly was no laughing matter, and the 1960s blight of redevelopment has since robbed this area of its regency elegance. (A.H.Barkway)

69. The tramcar on the left enters Grand Depot Road at the start of the one way section. The facing crossover in the foreground had been used in earlier days when the Royal Artillery held special memorial services at St.George's Garrison Church which is just visible behind the trees. On these occasions tram traffic was worked on a single line basis along Woolwich New Road. (J.C.Gillham)

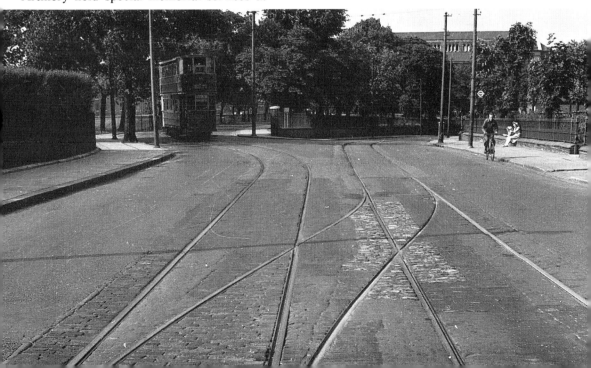

72. Car 186, originally from a batch built for Leyton Corporation and described in companion volume *Walthamstow and Leyton Tramways*, emerges from the southern end of Woolwich New Road. (C.Carter)

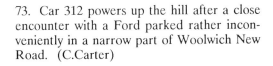

70. "Progress" in the form of a vast increase of traffic heading for a new approach road to the Woolwich Ferry has transformed this once pleasant thoroughfare into a fume filled race track. This is all in the future as we observe car 89 making its stately way along Grand Depot Road. (A.B.Cross)

71. The building to the left of car 577 forms part of the Royal Artillery Barracks which date from 1775. The tram stop opposite the Parade Ground is strategically placed on the wrong side of the road. Tram passengers were often treated to the spectacle of precision marching from army personnel, many of whom at this time were conscripts. Mistakes in drill from the "new boys" always drew a suitable reprimand from the accompanying sergeant! (C.Carter)

73. Car 312 powers up the hill after a close encounter with a Ford parked rather inconveniently in a narrow part of Woolwich New Road. (C.Carter)

74. The London bound and Woolwich bound tracks join up again outside St.Peter's Church and the infant and junior schools. Note the track work going on barely a week before the cessation of service. (J.C.Gillham)

75. This crossover near Anglesea Road once marked the end of the double trolley wires from Eltham. Trams proceeding to Woolwich would then lower one pole for the short journey to Beresford Square. The LCC measured the "three mile exclusion zone" from Greenwich Observatory to the inch! This rather impractical state of affairs was remedied on 16th February 1922 when the double overhead was extended right round the terminal loop. (J.C.Gillham)

36 Greenwich Church—New Bridge St., Blackfriars
via Deptford, Old Kent Road and Blackfriars Bridge.
THROUGH FARE 2½d.   RETURN FARE 4d.
Extended to WICKHAM LANE during busy hours.
WEEKDAYS From Greenwich Church First Car 9.23 am Last Car 11.54 pm
         Wickham Lane   7.25   9.2
         New Bridge Street   6.11
Last Car to Wickham Lane 7.39 ; Greenwich Ch. 11.9 pm ; New Cross 12.37 am
SUNDAYS extended to WICKHAM LANE after 12.0 noon.
                  First Car Last Car
From Greenwich Ch.   8.53 am   11.40 pm   (12.49 to New Cross)
  Wickham Lane   1.16 pm   11.2 pm
  New Bridge Street 8.15 am   12.9 am   (To Greenwich Ch.)
  New Bridge Street to
    Wickham Lane   12.3 pm   9.43 pm

38 WICKHAM LANE—WATERLOO BRIDGE
via Greenwich, Old Kent Road and Westminster Bridge.
THROUGH FARE 3d.   RETURN FARE 5d.
                  First Car Last Car
WEEKDAYS From Wickham Lane 6.56 am 10.35 pm (11.54 to New X.)
        Waterloo Bdg.   6.29   10.25   (12.8 am ,,)
SUNDAYS (extended to Bexley Heath)
      From Beresford Square 8.53   11.27
      Bexley Heath   10.35   10.21
      Waterloo Bridge 10.3   11.1 to Beresford Sq.

40 Abbey Wood—Waterloo Bridge (Victoria Embkt.)
via Woolwich, Greenwich and Kennington.
THROUGH FARE 3d.   RETURN FARE 5d.
WEEKDAYS From Abbey Wood   First Car 4.37 am Last Car 11.7 pm
        Waterloo Bdg.   5.16   10.35
SUNDAYS   Abbey Wood   8.22   10.37
        Waterloo Bridge   8.30   10.55

42 ABBEY WOOD—FREE FERRY, Woolwich
via McLeod Road, Plumstead Road and Beresford Square.
THROUGH FARE 2d.   RETURN FARE 3d.
WEEKDAYS From Abbey Wood First Car 4.19, 4.37 am Last Car 11.46 pm
        Free Ferry   5.3   12.10 am

44 BERESFORD SQ., Woolwich—ELTHAM
via Woolwich Common Road and Well Hall Road.
THROUGH FARE 2d.   RETURN FARE 3d.
WEEKDAYS From Beresford Square First Car 5.5 am Last Car 11.30 pm
        Eltham   5.22   11.52
SUNDAYS   Beresford Square   8.30   11.29
        Eltham   8.50   11.50

46 LEE GREEN—WATERLOO STATION
via Lewisham, New X, Peckham, Walworth Rd. & 'Elephant.'
THROUGH FARE 3d.   RETURN FARE 5d.
WEEKDAYS From Lee Green   First Car 5.1 pm   Last Car 11.51 pm
        Waterloo Stn.   5.40   11.52 (12.40 to New X)
SUNDAYS   Lee Green   8.58   11.30 pm
        Waterloo Stn.   8.32   11.35 (12.17 Lewisham)

List of services July 1915.

LAST TRAM WEEK
ON JULY 5 WE SAY GOODBYE TO LONDON

76. Although the trams imposed their own one way scheme, as the picture proves some motorists would disregard this and try to squeeze through regardless. The motorman of car 1407 keeps a wary eye out as a sister vehicle slips into Thomas Street. (A.J.Watkins)

77. The rails curve from Thomas Street into Green's End in front of some of the many small shops which were once a feature of this area of Woolwich. In modern times wholesale demolition of some of the properties hereabouts has resulted in a new open space for the centre of town. (J.C.Gillham)

78. We look along Green's End to the Arsenal Gate in the distance. A service 46 car is on the final stage of its journey from London and the existence of double trolley wires at this location means a date somewhere between 1922 and 1927. Note the 54 bus unloading, this route has been associated with Woolwich for many years. (J.H.Price Coll.)

79. Shoppers gather outside Sidney Ross near the corner of Powis Street and Green's End. Car 332 has halted for the zebra crossing and the motorman also looks round to check on any passengers alighting at the tram stop. (R.J.S.Wiseman)

80. This scene of Powis Street is taken from a postcard sent in June 1904. In the centre of the roadway is the narrow gauge horse tramway which was opened on 4th June 1881. Unfortunately this branch line off the main Plumstead to Greenwich route failed to attract enough paying customers and after 1883 the service was down to a single car every few weeks to maintain the company's running rights. (R.J.Harley Coll.)

81. Beresford Square with its street market was very much the heart of town. The trams added something extra - a vitality which was felt when a harassed motorman had to clear a passage through a throng of shoppers. The sound of tram gongs contrasting with the calls of the market traders is a cherished memory, it formed a movement in the symphony of London. (E.Course)

82. The central island in the Square served many purposes and had facilities for tram passengers and stall holders alike. It outlived both trams and trolleybuses and was finally demolished in the 1970s. (A.J.Watkins)

Extract from LT circular January 1936.

83. The one o'clock lunch time rush of Arsenal workers was an event and as such was guaranteed to attract the attention of postcard photographers. The horse tram company was alive to this potential increase in revenue and it instituted express cars to cope with the hordes of hungry men. Letters to the local press reported that ladies and well dressed individuals were normally excluded from such cars, in which case they resigned themselves to the walk! (J.H.Price Coll.)

84. No need of express horse cars now because the electric age has arrived. This view was taken around 1913 and shows cars on the Eltham and Abbey Wood services with their service numbers fixed on a metal plate under the canopy. The siding to the left of the island normally held a Bexley Council tram en route to Plumstead, Welling and Bexleyheath. (J.H.Price Coll.)

85. The date is now sometime around 1930 and we catch sight of car 1364 newly repainted in crimson livery. The siding for Bexley cars was removed during the First World War and from August 1918 they terminated on the east side of the Square. (J.B.Gent Coll.)

86. This view presents an interesting comparison with the previous picture. On the surface little seems to have changed, however, the transport world has moved on. Trolleybus overhead for routes 696 and 698 was erected in 1935 and the latest addition to the scene is the RTL diesel bus on route 53A.
(J.M.B.Bonell)

87. By the island shelter car 312 rests awhile before returning to Eltham. On these ex West Ham cars the top deck end window could be lowered for extra ventilation in warm weather. The track on which the tram is standing would remain in place for over thirty years after abandonment until it disappeared with the recent repaving associated with the new dual carriageway Plumstead Road scheme.
(J.C.Gillham)

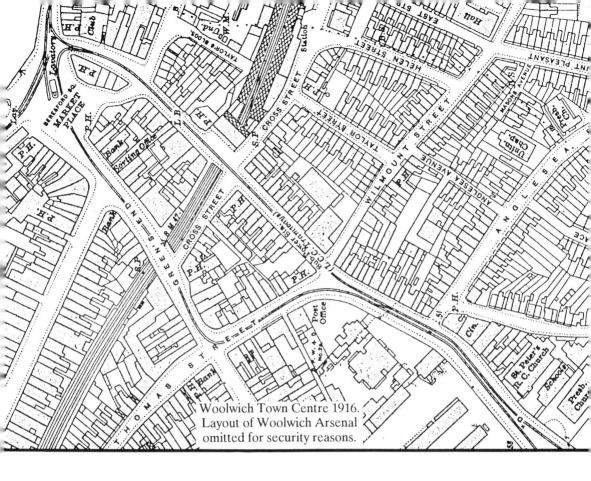

Woolwich Town Centre 1916.
Layout of Woolwich Arsenal
omitted for security reasons.

88. The connecting track to the Plumstead Road services 36, 38 and 40 was used for depot workings and shunting as seen here where car 88 has been eased forward to let the following 72 leave the terminus first. (A.J.Watkins)

89. A student of late twenties/early thirties fashion would find much of interest in this scene of Woolwich New Road by Beresford Square. On the right outside the Ordnance Arms hangs the green and white SOUTHERN ELECTRIC sign pointing the way to Woolwich Arsenal Station. A competing form of transport in the shape of car 1374 on service 46 is about to depart on its run to Southwark Bridge - a journey time of 64 minutes with a return fare of eightpence (3p).
(J.B.Gent Coll.)

90. The interlaced points at the entrance to Woolwich New Road were an object of study for trackwork specialists. The curves from Beresford Square and Plumstead Road were such that a conventional arrangement would have involved road widening and possible demolition of one of the two pubs facing the Square. (A.J.Watkins)

91. There is no need to rush to catch your tram as there'll be another one along in a minute. Heading the queue is car 2, the only reconditioned tram to make it to the very last day of the system. It was a frequent sight in the Woolwich area and was even rostered on Eltham local service 44 as well as the trunk routes to Central London. (R.B.Parr/NTM)

92. Back to double trolley days in Woolwich New Road with this mid 1920s scene, where we observe a car in the distance just about to pass the forecourt of Woolwich Arsenal Station. (J.H.Price Coll.)

93. In the days before double yellow lines and traffic wardens there was still plenty of space to park the family saloon whilst you nipped round the corner to the market or popped in the station to meet someone. (J.C.Gillham)

94. Car 2 again, this time on service 46 outside Woolwich Arsenal Station. The strange objects on the extreme left of the picture are portable traffic bollards which were employed by the Metropolitan Police. (D. Trevor Rowe)

95. Car 577 is caught by the camera at Woolwich, Perrott Street crossover just a few hundred yards east of Beresford Square. The conductress stands on the back fender; she is guiding the trolley rope to counter the risk of a dewirement. Unlike their rubber tyred replacements the trams were double ended and could reverse with a minimum of fuss. One assumes that the conductress has already flipped over the seat backs in preparation for the return journey. (A.J. Watkins)

BERESFORD STREET TO CHARLTON, PENHALL ROAD

96. We catch sight of two trams and a distant trolleybus on Beresford Street. To the right of car 86 are the queuing pens to cope with peak time passenger flows. To the left in front of the cinema is the 1944 curve which was laid to enable Eltham to Greenwich workman specials to go direct without reversing. (A.J.Watkins)

97. The Woolwich Ferry end of Beresford Street was typified by rather cramped road layouts. The double track occupies most of the carriageway and a convenient facing crossover has been installed to enable trams to pass parked vehicles. This scene has now totally vanished due to road widening. (A.J.Watkins)

98. Embodying the philosophy "its never too late to learn", car 1019 offers its services for trainee motorman as it takes the tight bend from Beresford Street into Market Hill. (A.J.Watkins)

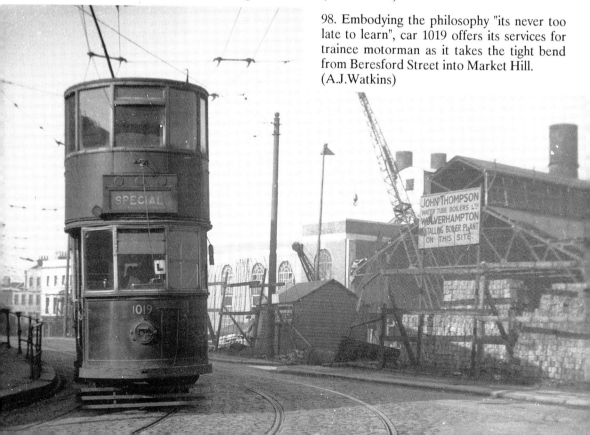

99. We look in the opposite direction to the previous photograph to observe former Croydon Corporation car 377 as it makes its way past war damaged properties. (C.Carter)

100. In Market Hill car 1862 on an enthusiasts' special has just traversed the change pit and it now gets ready to proceed on the conduit. In the background a brace of buses on route 75 stand at the original Woolwich Ferry trolley-bus terminus. The date is 22nd April 1951. (G.F.Ashwell)

101. Several trams wait in the High Street for the traffic queue to cross from Hare Street to the Woolwich Ferry Approach. The opportunity has been taken on both cars to raise the trolley pole in advance of the change pit. The motorman will then switch over to draw current from the overhead before shooting the plough further up the road. (C.Carter)

102. The wall of the Royal Dockyard Woolwich forms a backdrop to car 305. The Dockyard itself has a long historical pedigree stretching back to Tudor times. More recently in 1909/10 the LCC had to rebuild a large section of the wall in connection with road widening for the new electric tramway. (R.J.Harley Coll.)

ROUTE 36/38 | **Abbey Wood – Woolwich – New Cross – Elephant & Castle – Savoy St.** | P.M. times are in heavy figures

Via McLeod Road, Basildon Road, Plumstead High Street, Plumstead Road, Beresford Street, Woolwich High Street, Woolwich Church Street, Woolwich Road, Trafalgar Road, Romney Road, Nelson Street, London Street, Greenwich Road, Deptford Broadway, New Cross Road, Old Kent Road, New Kent Road, London Road. Route 36 via Blackfriars Road, Blackfriars Bridge, Victoria Embankment (return via Westminster Bridge, Westminster Bridge Road.) Route 38 via London Road, Westminster Bridge Road, Westminster Bridge, Victoria Embankment, Blackfriars Bridge

RAILWAY STATIONS SERVED : Abbey Wood, Plumstead, near Woolwich Arsenal, Charlton, Greenwich, New Cross, New Cross Gate, Elephant and Castle, Blackfriars, Temple, Charing Cross, Westminster, Lambeth North

Service interval : EACH ROUTE. WEEKDAYS 6 mins. (evening 24 mins.), SUNDAY 10 mins. (evening 24 mins.) (Additional peak hour service on Weekdays between Abbey Wood and New Cross, every 8 mins.).

	WEEKDAYS First						SUNDAY First					DAILY Last				
			†		*		*		†	*	*	*	SOT	SO*	SXT	SX*	S⊠X	S⊠0
ABBEY WOOD	....	....	4 34	5 22	....	....	5 25	5 57	A6 1	6 20	7 15	8 29	8 41	8 53	9 5	10 29	10 36
Woolwich *Beresford Square*	....	....	4 49	5 38	....	....	5 41	6 13	6 9	6 36	7 31	8 45	8 57	9 9	9 21	10 45	10 52
Woolwich Road *Blackwall Lane*	4 16	....	5 4	5 54	....	5 30	‡5 49	X5 50	6 29	6 52	7 46	9 1	9 13	9 25	9 37	11 1	11 8
New Cross Gate	4 31	4 41	5 20	6 11	4 12	5 49	6 0	....	6 46	6 42	7 9	9 18	9 30	9 42	9 54	11 18	11 25
Elephant & Castle	4 47	4 57	5 36	6 27	4 27	6 4	6 16	....	7 2	6 58	7 25	9 34	9 46	9 58	10 10	....	....
Blackfriars *John Carpenter Street*..	....	5 6	5 46	....	4 34	....	6 26	....	....	7 8	7 35	....	9 56	....	10 20	....	....
VICTORIA EMBANK. *Savoy St.*.	5 0	¶5 12	5 50	6 41	4 36	....	6 30	....	7 16	....	....	9 48	10 0	10 12	10 24	....	....

												⊠0*	⊠X*	⊠0*	⊠0	†	
		*	†		*		*	†									
VICTORIA EMBANK. *Savoy St.*..	....	5 0	¶5 14	5 42	4 37	....	4 48	6 31	8 24	....	....	9 24	9 48	9 48	....	10 0	....
Blackfriars *John Carpenter Street*..	....	5 3	5 20	....	4 39	4 44	4 50	6 35	....	....	....	9 28	9 52	9 52	....	....	....
Elephant & Castle	....	5 13	5 30	5 56	4 46	4 51	4 57	6 45	8 34	....	....	9 38	10 2	10 2	....	10 14	....
New Cross Gate	3 50	5 29	5 46	6 12	5 0	5 5	5 11	7 1	8 49	....	....	9 54	10 18	10 18	10 19	10 30	....
Woolwich Road *Blackwall Lane* ..	4 7	5 46	6 3	6 29	....	5 19	5 29	7 18	9 3	....	....	10 11	10 35	....	10 36	10 47	....
Woolwich *Beresford Square*	4 23	6 2	6 19	6 45	....	5 34	....	7 34	9 18.	....	....	10 27	10 51	....	10 52	11 3	....
ABBEY WOOD	4 38	6 18	6 35	7 1	....	5 50	....	7 49	9 33	....	....	10 43	11 7	....	11 8	11 19	....

LATE JOURNEYS, SATURDAY EXCEPTED

Abbey Wood to Savoy Street *9 37 p.m. | Savoy Street to New Cross *10 12, *10 26, *10 58 p.m.

A–Time at Wickham Lane. SO–Sat. only. SX–Sat. excepted. ⊠X–Sun. excepted. ⊠0–Sun. only. S⊠0–Sat. and Sun only. S⊠X–Sat. and Sun. excepted. X–Time at Charlton *Church Lane.* ¶–Time at Charing Cross. ‡–Time at Greenwich *Church.* *–Via Blackfriars. †–Via Westminster.

ALL NIGHT ROUTE	**New Cross Gate – Camberwell Green – Elephant – Savoy Street**									
	SATURDAY NIGHT, SUNDAY MORNING EXCEPTED							T–Time at St. Georges Church.		

NEW CROSS GT.	12 15	12 45	1 15	1 45	2 15	2 45	3 15	3 45	4 15	4 45	5 27
Camberwell Green	12 26	12 56	1 26	1 56	2 26	2 56	3 26	3 56	4 26	4 56	5 41
Savoy Street	12 45	1 15	1 45	2 15	2 45	3 15	3 45	4 15	4 45	5 15	T5 57
CHARING X Stn.	..	..	..	..	..	..	..	..	..	5 17	..

CHARING X Stn.											5 17	
Savoy Street	12 45	1 15	1 45	2 15	2 45	3 15	3 45	4 15	4 45	5 19	T6 0
Camberwell Green	1 4	1 34	2 4	2 34	3 4	3 34	4 4	4 34	5 4	5 38	6 16
NEW CROSS GT.	1 15	1 45	2 15	2 45	3 15	3 45	4 15	4 45	5 15	5 49	6 30

Extract from LT timetable December 1943.

103. We have now crossed from the old Metropolitan Borough of Woolwich into the neighbouring Borough of Greenwich. Here on Woolwich Road by Penhall Road work has started on laying the connecting track to the new scrap sidings. On this dull January day in 1950 the fate of the remaining tramcars has been well and truly sealed. (J.H.Meredith)

104. The sun shines on a melancholy sight as another victim shoots its plough for the last time to enter Penhall Yard. Obviously it was much cheaper to use overhead wires than to lay new conduit tracks into the scrapyard. (C.Carter)

105. Traction poles line the perimeter of the sidings which will witness car 1656 being set ablaze on 2nd October 1950, and from then on the grisly task will gather momentum until car 179 finally meets its Waterloo on 29th January 1953. (J.H.Meredith)

Extract from L.C.C. Guide 1911.

Waterloo Bridge to Blackwall Tunnel and Woolwich-road (circular route) and Waterloo Station to New Cross (Electric Traction).

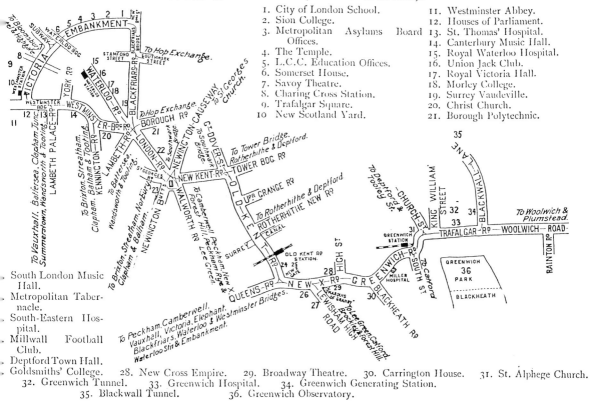

1. City of London School.
2. Sion College.
3. Metropolitan Asylums Board Offices.
4. The Temple.
5. L.C.C. Education Offices.
6. Somerset House.
7. Savoy Theatre.
8. Charing Cross Station.
9. Trafalgar Square.
10. New Scotland Yard.
11. Westminster Abbey.
12. Houses of Parliament.
13. St. Thomas' Hospital.
14. Canterbury Music Hall.
15. Royal Waterloo Hospital.
16. Union Jack Club.
17. Royal Victoria Hall.
18. Morley College.
19. Surrey Vaudeville.
20. Christ Church.
21. Borough Polytechnic.

South London Music Hall.
Metropolitan Tabernacle.
South-Eastern Hospital.
Millwall Football Club.
Deptford Town Hall.
Goldsmiths' College.

28. New Cross Empire. 29. Broadway Theatre. 30. Carrington House. 31. St. Alphege Church.
32. Greenwich Tunnel. 33. Greenwich Hospital. 34. Greenwich Generating Station.
35. Blackwall Tunnel. 36. Greenwich Observatory.

106. Some efficiency was added to the official vandalism by the use of this traverser which moved doomed trams sideways to various holding tracks. Some rather forlorn relics including a maximum traction truck lie abandoned in the background. (C.Carter)

This receipt was issued by George Cohen who ran the scrapping operation at Penhall Road. A sum of twelve shillings and sixpence (62p) secured three gongs and a single tram seat.

| | GEORGE COHEN SONS & COMPANY LTD. | This No. must appear on our account ☞ D19 | Nᵒ 4672 |

GEORGE COHEN SONS & COMPANY LTD.

This No. must appear on our account ☞ **D 19**   Nᵒ   **4672**

BROADWAY CHAMBERS, HAMMERSMITH, LONDON, W.6.

Job at *L YE Charlton*

Goods Agent

Please despatch to :- *Mᵒ Catchpole*   8.1.51 19

O.R. Rates where applicable.
Carriage to our Account.

TRUCK No. or CONVEYANCE	MATERIAL	TONS	CWTS.	QRS.	LB
	3 Gongs @ 2/6 Each				
	1 Single Seat	5/-			
	12/6	*P Barrett*			

This copy to accompany loads sent by ROAD, direct to CUSTOMER or DEPOT.

Foreman.

Form No. 118

107. One special casualty of Penhall Road was this horse drawn tower wagon which was built by Rawlinson. It was probably left behind by the contractor after construction work for the LCC. Many of these old type wagons survived into the motor age by being used in depots for repainting roof girders, for cleaning roof glass, or for gaining access to light bulbs. (J.H.Meredith)

CHARLTON CENTRAL REPAIR DEPOT
TO EAST GREENWICH

108. At the entrance to Charlton Works we encounter two ex West Ham trams which served as staff cars for LT employees. This short roadway was subsequently named Felltram Way in honour of A.L.C.Fell the former LCC General Manager.
(R.J.Harley Coll.)

←————————

109. The craftsmen at Charlton formed a skilled elite and it must have been with particular pride that they produced car 795 seen here outside the works. The date is February 1932 and this car is painted in experimental aluminium/grey livery ready to go out on the road. A further view of this vehicle is contained in companion volume *Embankment and Waterloo Tramways*. (LCC official photo)

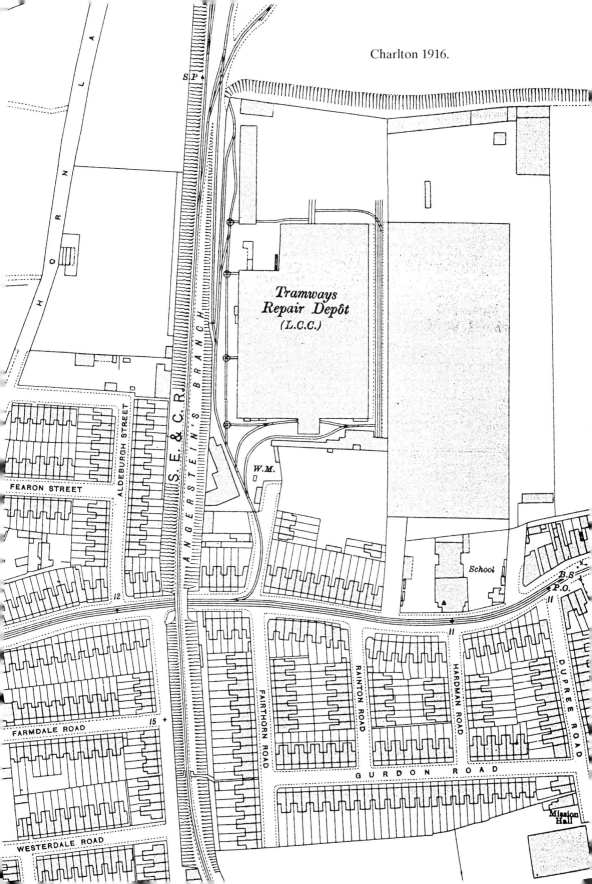

Charlton 1916.

Tramways
Repair Depôt
(L.C.C.)

S.E. & C. R. J.

ANGERSTEIN'S BRANCH

HORN LA

S P

W.M.

School

B.S

P.O.

ALDEBURGH STREET

FEARON STREET

FARMDALE ROAD

WESTERDALE ROAD

FAIRTHORN ROAD

RAINTON ROAD

HARDMAN ROAD

DUPREE ROAD

GURDON ROAD

Mission Hall

12

15

11

11

110. We view the main building from the adjacent railway embankment. Two small ex LCC stores vehicles have been loaded with wheelsets for their daily journey from Charlton to one of the remaining depots. On the left is one of the staff cars and in the foreground a couple of railway wagons prove the fact that the tracks within the works yard could be used by both railway and tramway vehicles. In LCC days cars were shunted around the works by an Andrew Barclay 0-4-0 saddle tank steam locomotive. (J.H.Meredith)

111. A youthful Richard Elliott stands at the controls of car 1912, part of the new E3 class which were delivered in 1930. This tram would later be fitted with a driver's windscreen. (R.Elliott)

Baptist Chapel, Woolwich Road

←—————

112. Horse meets electric in 1909 at the corner of Tunnel Avenue and Woolwich Road. The narrow gauge horse trams operated from a temporary depot in Tunnel Avenue. Meanwhile standard gauge electric car 342 prepares to depart for Waterloo Station.
(R.J.Harley Coll.)

114. We finish our trip along Woolwich Road in the company of car 1490 which is pictured near the junction with Blackwall Lane.
(J.H.Price Coll.)

←—————

113. Car 352 passes the Baptist Chapel at Kemsing Road shortly after the Blackwall Lane to Tunnel Avenue section opened on 10th June 1906. Passengers wishing to continue their journey to Charlton and Woolwich would have to transfer to the horse tram which can be glimpsed in the distance. (J.H.Price Coll.)

ROLLING STOCK

Class H cars 01-04. These vehicles were ordered in 1905 as water tank cars to keep the dust down along the tram tracks. Another function of these trams was to act as grinders to alleviate rail corrugations. For this purpose they were fitted with carborundum blocks either side of the trucks. The blocks could then be screwed down on to the surface of the rail to smoothe out corrugations. Each car was dual fitted for conduit and overhead; car 01 was given an extra trolley pole to work the double trolley Eltham route. All four members of class H passed to London Transport on 1st July 1933 and they continued to serve into the post war years.

115. Pictured towards the end of its working life, car 02 rests before being sent out on another trackwork duty. Note the ladder which was used for access to the main inlet of the water tank. The accompanying drawing has been kindly supplied by Terry Russell. (R.Elliott)

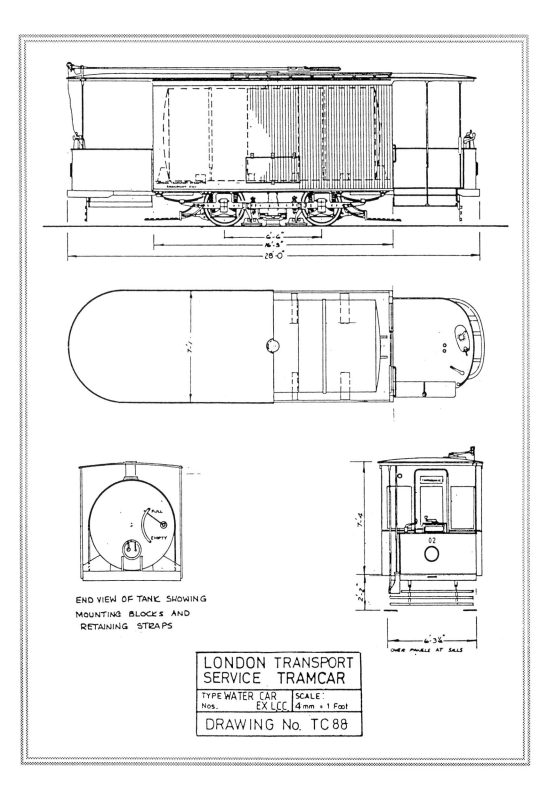

END VIEW OF TANK SHOWING
MOUNTING BLOCKS AND
RETAINING STRAPS

LONDON TRANSPORT SERVICE TRAMCAR		
TYPE WATER CAR Nos. EX LCC	SCALE: 4 mm = 1 Foot	
DRAWING No. TC 88		

SECTION BOXES

Section boxes or feeder pillars were situated at roughly half mile intervals and their function was to supply current at 550 volts to either the conduit or the overhead. As the name suggests, they contained switches so that sections of tramway could be isolated from the power supply in case of emergencies. Many boxes survived the tramways only to be removed in the late fifties and early sixties as local councils "tidied up" pavements.

FEEDERS

The feeder system includes all the cables necessary to distribute the current from the generating station or substation to the working conductors; in the overhead system it consists of the trolley wires and the track rails. In compliance with the Board of Trade regulations, the trolley wire is divided into ½-mile sections insulated from one another, and the connection with the feeder system is usually made at the centre or ends of each section.

In the conduit system, which has an insulated return, the negative feeders are duplicates of the positive feeders; but in the overhead system, which has an earthed return, the negative feeder system differs from the positive, and requires separate consideration. In Great Britain, feeder cables are laid underground, but in America, on the Continent, and in the Colonies they are run overhead. They usually follow the line of track, but considerable saving may sometimes be effected by taking a short cut between the power station and the feeding point; this means not only a saving in the cost of the feeder, but also in the watts lost in transmission. Any of the standard types of underground mains may be used for feeders.

Feeder Pillars.—The positive feeder terminates on a small switchboard placed in a cast-iron box, called a feeder, or switch, pillar, which is placed on the footpath near the point at which connection is to be made to the trolley wire. The short feeders connecting the main feeder with the trolley wire are called line taps, or side feed-cables. They are usually drawn inside one of the poles used for supporting the trolley wire; and from the pole they pass along either the bracket arm or span wire to a feeder ear attached to the overhead wire. These line taps are connected to a feeder bus-bar in the switch pillar through trolley switches, which are used when necessary for cutting the current off the overhead wire.

A typical tramway feeder pillar, arranged for feeding at the section insulators, is shown in Fig. 43, (a) being the front view

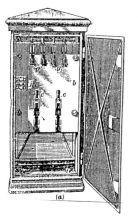
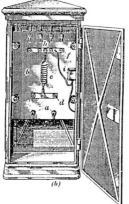

Fig. 43

and (b) the back view. The incoming feeders from the power station are connected to the terminals a, which pass through the slate slab b to the lower terminals of the switches c. When these switches are closed, they connect the feeders to the bus-bar d, which is connected through the choking coil e of the lightning arrester to the bus-bar f. The bottom contacts of the trolley switches g are connected to this bus-bar f, and the top contacts are provided with sockets h, into which the side feed-cables are sweated. Any side feed-cable can thus be connected to the feeder bus-bar by closing its switch. A lightning arrester i is connected to the bus-bar f, while a terminal board j is provided for telephone or pilot wires. The feeder pillar is fitted with doors at front and back, so that the switches and connections are easily accessible. The doors are kept locked, so that no unauthorized persons can have access to the connections.

116. This is the standard LCC model doing duty at Newington Green. The smaller box on the top contained a telephone vital for communicating traffic information to the local inspector. The whole contraption was painted dark green. Not all these feeder pillars were to be found where you might expect them, and the author remembers one at the Royal Standard, Blackheath some distance from the nearest tram route. (D.A.Thompson)

117. This is the slim, elegant MET version which once existed at Golders Green. Note the rather stylish monogram on the front of the feeder pillar. (D.A.Thompson)

118. The London Transport regime brought this functional 1930s design to Lee High Road. This box lasted until the 1960s. (J.C.Gillham)

119. This is another LT example based on the previous standard LCC model. Here at Lee Green change pit the attendant could be reached on the phone by dialling OT 135. (J.C.Gillham)

FINALE

120. The first generation of London's trams has now gone for good. On 19th April 1953 one of the replacing buses accelerates past the road-works necessary for the removal of the tram-lines. In a short time the remaining traction poles will also be uprooted in favour of new Woolwich Borough Council lamp standards. (E.Course)

MP Middleton Press

Easebourne Lane, Midhurst. West Sussex. GU29 9AZ   Tel: 01730 813169 Fax: 01730 812601

. . . . . Write or telephone for our latest list . . . . .

BRANCH LINES
Branch Line to Allhallows
Branch Lines to Alton
Branch Lines around Ascot
Branch Line to Bude
Branch Lines around Canterbury
Branch Lines to East Grinstead
Branch Lines around Effingham Jn
Branch Lines to Exmouth
Branch Line to Fairford
Branch Line to Hawkhurst
Branch Lines to Horsham
Branch Lines around Huntingdon
Branch Lines to Ilfracombe
Branch Line to Lyme Regis
Branch Line to Lynton
Branch Lines around March
Branch Lines around Midhurst
Branch Lines to Newport
Branch Line to Padstow
Branch Lines around Portmadoc 1923-46
Branch Lines around Porthmadog 1954-94
Branch Lines to Seaton & Sidmouth
Branch Line to Selsey
Branch Lines around Sheerness
Branch Line to Southwold
Branch Line to Swanage
Branch Line to Tenterden
Branch Lines to Torrington
Branch Lines to Tunbridge Wells
Branch Line to Upwell
Branch Lines around Weymouth

LONDON SUBURBAN RAILWAYS
Caterham and Tattenham Corner
Clapham Jn. to Beckenham Jn.
Crystal Palace and Catford Loop
Holborn Viaduct to Lewisham
London Bridge to Addiscombe
Mitcham Junction Lines
South London Line
West Croydon to Epsom
Willesden Junction to Richmond
Wimbledon to Epsom

STEAMING THROUGH
Steaming through Cornwall
Steaming through East Sussex
Steaming through the Isle of Wight
Steaming through Surrey
Steaming through West Hants
Steaming through West Sussex

GREAT RAILWAY ERAS
Ashford from Steam to Eurostar
Festiniog in the Fifties

COUNTRY BOOKS
Brickmaking in Sussex
East Grinstead Then and Now

SOUTH COAST RAILWAYS
Ashford to Dover
Bournemouth to Weymouth
Brighton to Eastbourne
Brighton to Worthing
Chichester to Portsmouth
Dover to Ramsgate
Hastings to Ashford
Ryde to Ventnor
Worthing to Chichester

SOUTHERN MAIN LINES
Bromley South to Rochester
Charing Cross to Orpington
Crawley to Littlehampton
Dartford to Sittingbourne
East Croydon to Three Bridges
Epsom to Horsham
Exeter to Barnstaple
Exeter to Tavistock
Faversham to Dover
Haywards Heath to Seaford
London Bridge to East Croydon
Orpington to Tonbridge
Sittingbourne to Ramsgate
Swanley to Ashford
Three Bridges to Brighton
Tonbridge to Hastings
Victoria to Bromley South
Waterloo to Windsor
Woking to Southampton
Yeovil to Exeter

COUNTRY RAILWAY ROUTES
Andover to Southampton
Bath to Evercreech Junction
Bournemouth to Evercreech Jn
Burnham to Evercreech Junction
Croydon to East Grinstead
East Kent Light Railway
Fareham to Salisbury
Guildford to Redhill
Porthmadog to Blaenau
Reading to Basingstoke
Reading to Guildford
Redhill to Ashford
Salisbury to Westbury
Strood to Paddock Wood
Taunton to Barnstaple
Westbury to Bath
Woking to Alton

TROLLEYBUS CLASSICS
Croydon's Trolleybuses
Woolwich & Dartford Trolleybuses

TRAMWAY CLASSICS
Aldgate & Stepney Tramways
Bournemouth & Poole Tramways
Brighton's Tramways
Bristol's Tramways
Camberwell & W. Norwood Tramway
Croydon's Tramways
Dover's Tramways
East Ham & West Ham Tramways
Embankment & Waterloo Tramways
Exeter & Taunton Tramways
Greenwich & Dartford Tramways
Hampstead & Highgate Tramways
Hastings Tramways
Ilford & Barking Tramways
Kingston & Wimbledon Tramways
Lewisham & Catford Tramways
Maidstone & Chatham Tramways
North Kent Tramways
Portsmouth's Tramways
Southampton Tramways
Southend-on-sea Tramways
Thanet's Tramways
Victoria & Lambeth Tramways
Walthamstow & Leyton Tramways
Wandsworth & Battersea Tramways

OTHER RAILWAY BOOKS
Garraway Father & Son
Industrial Railways of the South East
London Chatham & Dover Railway
South Eastern Railway
War on the Line

MILITARY BOOKS
Battle over Portsmouth
Battle Over Sussex 1940
Blitz Over Sussex 1941-42
Bognor at War
Bombers over Sussex 1943-45
Military Defence of West Sussex

WATERWAY ALBUMS
Hampshire Waterways
Kent and East Sussex Waterways
London to Portsmouth Waterway
West Sussex Waterways

BUS BOOK
Eastbourne Bus Story

SOUTHERN RAILWAY ● VIDEOS ●
Memories of the Hayling Island Branch
Memories of the Lyme Regis Branch
War on the Line